North Cornwall: **Tea Shop** Walks

First published 2025 in by:

Northern Eye Books Limited
Northern Eye Books, Tattenhall, Cheshire CH3 9PX
© Northern Eye Books Limited 2025

ISBN 978-1-914589-18-8

Text: *Vivienne Crow*

Series editor: *Tony Bowerman*

Photographs: *Vivienne Crow, Boscastle Farm Shop, Cherry Trees Café, Café Q, The Hub, Adobestock, Dreamstime, Shutterstock, Alamy*

Design: *Carl Rogers and Laura Hodgkinson*

Vivienne Crow has asserted her rights under the Copyright, Designs and Patents Act, 1988 to be identified as the author of this work. All rights reserved

A CIP catalogue record for this book is available from the British Library.

Printed in the UK on woodland-friendly FSC stock

www.northerneyebooks.co.uk

 @northerneyebooks
@england_coast_path
@viviennecrow

 @northerneyeboo
@viviennecrow2

 @northerneyebooks

*For sales enquiries, please call 01928 723 744
Or email: tony@northerneyebooks.co.uk*

Important Advice: The routes described in this book are undertaken at the reader's own risk. Walkers should take into account their level of fitness, wear suitable footwear and clothing, and carry food and water. It is also advisable to take the relevant OS map with you in case you get lost and leave the area covered by our maps.

Whilst every care has been taken to ensure the accuracy of the route directions, the publishers cannot accept responsibility for errors or omissions, or for changes in the details given. Nor can the publisher and copyright owners accept responsibility for any consequences arising from the use of this book.

If you find any inaccuracies in either the text or maps, please write or email us at the address above. Thank you.

This book contains mapping data licensed from the Ordnance Survey with the permission of the Controller of Her Majesty's Stationery Office. © Crown copyright 2025 All rights reserved. Licence number AC0000833184

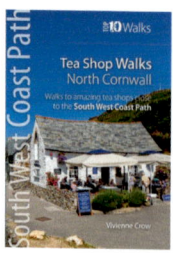

Cover: *Tea Room, Boscastle (Walk 3)*

Contents

South West Coast Path 4

Top 10 Walks: Tea Shop walks 6

1 | Widemouth Bay Café, *Bude* 8

2 | The Cabin Café, *Crackington Haven* 12

3 | Boscastle Farm Shop & Café, *Boscastle* .. 18

4 | Charlie's, *Tintagel* 24

5 | Woods Café, *Cardinham Woods* 30

6 | Cherry Trees, *Padstow* 36

7 | Beach Stores & Café, *Trevone* 42

8 | Café Q, *St Agnes Head* 48

9 | The Hub, *Portreath* 54

10 | Dog & Rabbit Café, *Cape Cornwall* 58

Useful Information 64

South West Coast Path

Running for 630 miles from Minehead in Somerset, around the tip of Land's End and back to South Haven Point at the mouth of Poole Harbour in Dorset, the **South West Coast Path** is one of Britain's longest National Trails. Bordered by the Bristol and English channels and looking out to the open Atlantic, it encompasses some of England's most spectacular and wildest coastline, where the diversity of plant, animal and insect life can be stunning. The seas, coves and surrounding hinterland has been a dramatic setting for a gloriously rich history, which have inspired countless tales of romance, drama and intrigue.

This series of Top Ten Walks explores highlights along the way; showcasing its natural beauty, wildlife and heritage and provoking imagination. Who knows, you may be inspired to come back to tackle the complete trail.

Ruined Wheal Prosper engine house on the cliffs at Rinsey Head near Porthleven

Tea Shops in North Cornwall

A walk on the North Cornwall coast without a visit to a tea shop is like Ant without Dec or fish without chips. What could be better than sitting down to afternoon tea—jam, first, of course!—at the end of a lovely walk along the crest of roller-coaster cliffs? Or tucking into a Cornish pasty while gazing out at a beautiful sandy bay? And you won't just find the time-honoured favourites; the cafés and tea shops of north Cornwall also serve up tasty brunches, vegan lunches and gluten-free cakes all washed down with excellent artisan coffees, local beers and even tea grown in the county. Modern or traditional, you'll find it here.

"Tea would arrive, the cakes squatting on cushions of cream, toast in a melting shawl of butter, cups agleam…"

Gerald Durrell

TOP 10 Walks: Cafés, Tea Shops and Bistros

THE TEN TEA SHOPS, CAFÉS AND BISTROS featured have been chosen partly because of the excellent walking that can be enjoyed from their doors and partly because of the fare and ambience they offer. They occupy beach, village, cliff-top and woodland locations. The walks themselves stretch almost the entire length of the coast—from Bude down to Cape Cornwall, just a few miles short of Land's End. As well as cliff-top walking, they take in sandy bays, hidden valleys, riverside paths and wildflower-filled woods as well as the fabulous viewpoints and heritage sites that help make Cornwall such a special place.

Widemouth Bay Café
Bude
page 8

The Cabin Café
Crackington Haven
page 12

Boscastle Farm Shop & Café, Boscastle
page 18

Charlie's
Tintagel
page 24

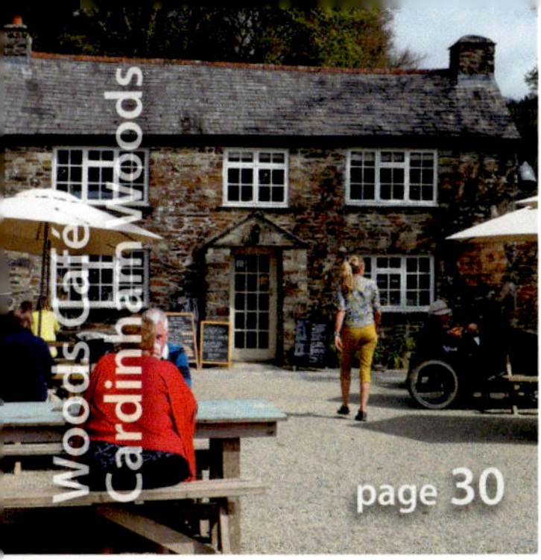
Woods Café
Cardinham Woods
page 30
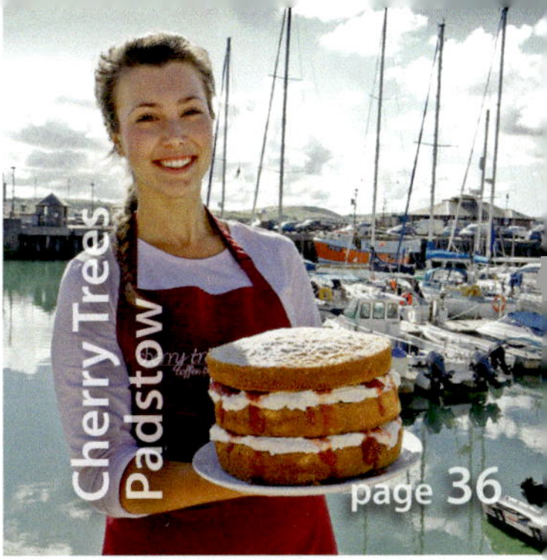
Cherry Trees
Padstow
page 36
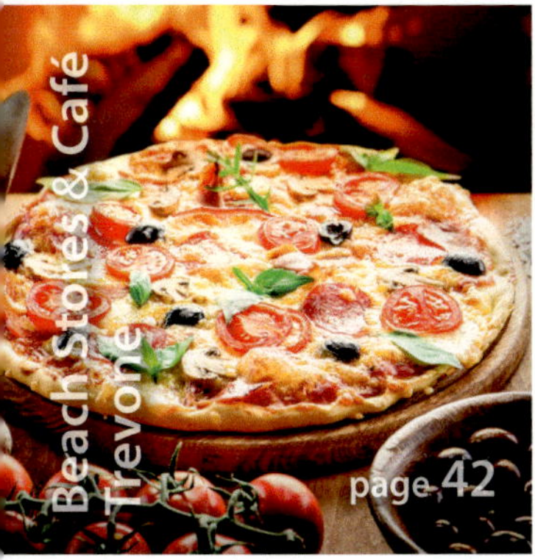
Beach Stores & Café
Trevone
page 42
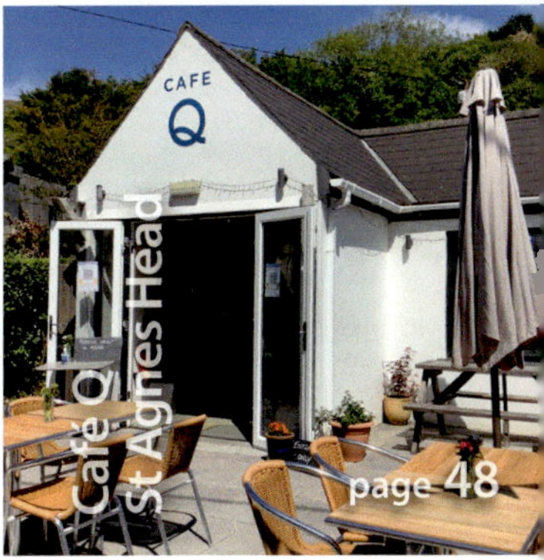
CAFE
Q
Café Q
St Agnes Head
page 48
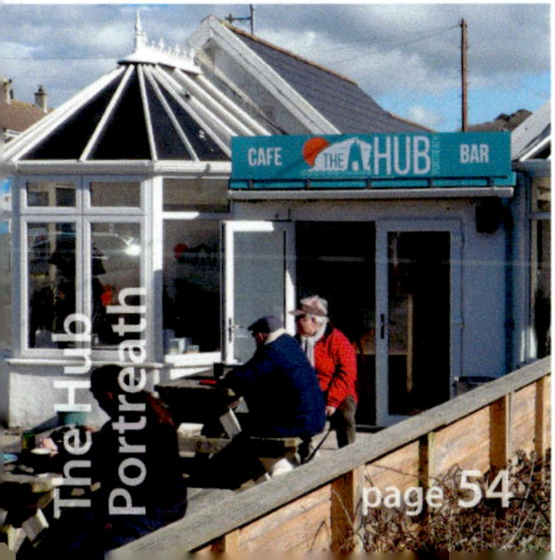
CAFE
THE HUB
BAR
The Hub
Portreath
page 54
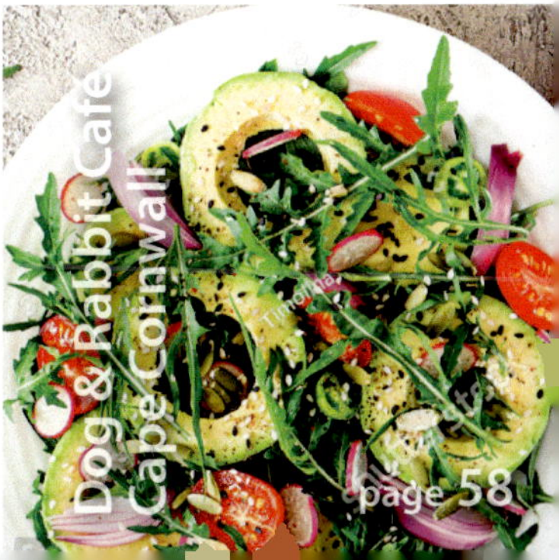
Dog & Rabbit Café
Cape Cornwall
page 58

A warm welcome at the Widemouth Bay Café

WIDEMOUTH BAY AND BUDE

walk 1

Widemouth Bay Café

After an easy stroll along low cliffs, walkers join a canal tow path in Bude

What to expect:
Dunes; low cliffs; surfaced tow path; fields

Distance/Time: 10 kilometres/6½miles. Allow 2½ - 3 hours

Start: Pay-and-display car park beside Widemouth Bay Café

Grid ref: SS 199 024

Ordnance Survey Map: Explorer 111, *Bude, Boscastle & Tintagel*

Café: Widemouth Bay Café, Marine Drive, Widemouth Bay EX23 0AH | 01288 361927 | www.widemouthbaycafe.co.uk

Walk outline: Surfers and dog-walkers aren't the only ones to flock to Widemouth Bay; geologists and fossil hunters come here too. Shales and sandstone dominate, creating interesting folds on the foreshore platform and friable cliffs, where persistent erosion frequently reveals fossils. Gaze down on the scene as you head north along the low cliffs to Bude. From this pleasant seaside town, a canal towpath makes a great contrast to the outward route, with bird's-eye views of the bay.

No matter what time of day you visit, this vibrant café is always busy with surfers, families and dog-walkers. If you can't get a table inside, there are lots outside too and a hatch for take-aways.

Local crab cakes

▶ The Widemouth Bay Café at a glance

Open: Daily, 9.30am-5pm
Food and specialities: All-day breakfasts, including pancakes; hot meals including crab cakes and various burgers; sandwiches (gluten-free available), paninis and pasties; children's menu
Beverages: Various teas and Illy coffee; thick shakes and smoothies; Luscombe organic soft drinks
Outside: Large outdoor dining area
Dogs: Well-behaved dogs welcome

The Walk

1. Walk to the end of the **car park** furthest from the **café**, cross the **bridge** and keep to the seaward side of the dunes. After a short section along the back of the beach, join a more solid path with a bench beside it. This passes to the right of a cottage and crosses two driveways.

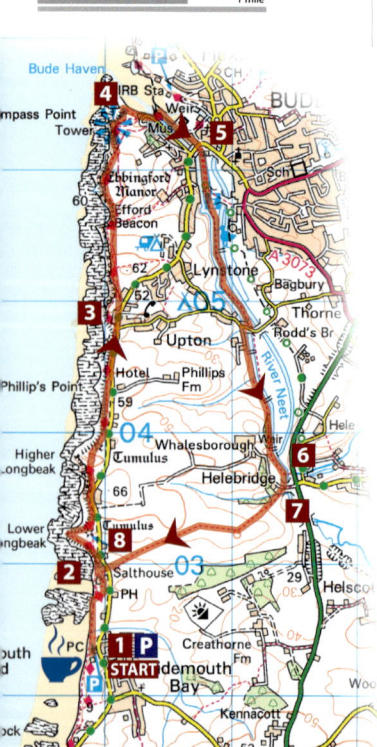

2. A few strides beyond a bench, fork left to reach the headland of **Lower Longbeak**. From the tip, marked by an arrangement of rocks, head back inland along the northern side. Bear left at a fork to stay on the cliffs. Beyond the **'Phillips' Point Nature Reserve'** sign, follow the clear path parallel with the road. Reaching a roadside sign for Upton Cross B&B, continue on the pavement for 190m.

3. Drawing level with a house called **Rough Down** on the right, turn left through a hedge gap. Return to the cliffs and climb to a gate. Once through this, drop to another gate before climbing left to the trig pillar at **Efford Beacon**. Bude is clearly visible. After the next gate, the path eases its way down to the octagonal **Storm Tower** at **Compass Point**, built as a coastguard refuge in the 1830s. Swing down with the cliffs to meet an asphalt path. Turn right.

4. At the bottom, descend the steps on the left and bear right along the asphalt above the beach. Turn left through the wall gap, descend steps and cross the **lock gate footbridge** to join the **canalside path**.

5. At the road in **Bude**, turn right and cross over to rejoin the **tow path**. After a green gate, turn right to cross the canal and then go left along the tow path.

6. Soon after the **Whalesborough Weir**, the waterway splits, with a **footbridge**

© Crown copyright and/or database right. All rights reserved. Licence number AC0000833184

Sunset over the beach at Widemouth Bay

across one arm. Ignoring this, keep straight ahead. Turn right along a lane, then, near some **information panels**, bear left and through the kissing-gate.

7. The right-of-way, unclear now, swings right (south-west). After a gate, cross the field, walking in the same direction as before. Beyond another gate, walk beside the hedgerow on the left. In the next field, head gently downhill, enjoying views of the bay below. Dropping into a final field, continue downhill beside the fence on your right, later swinging left to meet the road via a farm gate.

8. Cross over. Take the right-hand of the two tracks opposite and turn left just before the cottage to retrace your steps to the car park to complete the walk. ♦

Bude Canal

The Bude Canal was built to transport shell-rich sand from the coast to be used as fertiliser on farmland along the Devon and Cornwall border. It was unusual in that it used a system of inclined planes, along which wheeled boats would be hauled by chains – climbing a total of 132 metres along the canal's 56-kilometre length. The lock at Bude itself is one of only two sea locks in Britain.

The Cabin Café overlooks the beach at Crackington Haven

CRACKINGTON HAVEN

walk 2

The Cabin Café

A delightful woodland stroll followed by a hike along the top of dramatic, undulating cliffs

What to expect:
Woodland; farm paths; quiet lanes; cliffs

Distance/Time: 14 kilometres/9 miles. Allow 4¾-5¼ hours

Start: Pay-and-display car park in lowest part of Crackington Haven

Grid ref: SX 143 967

Ordnance Survey Map: Explorer 111, *Bude, Boscastle & Tintagel*

Café: The Cabin Café, Crackington Haven, Bude EX23 0JG | 01840 230238 | www.cabincafecrackington.co.uk

Walk outline: A walk of two halves. Much of the first part weaves its way in and out of woodland, some carpeted with bluebells in springtime. The highlight is the Woodland Trust's Millook Valley, cloaked in oak, ash and sycamore. Beyond Millook Haven, the walk takes on a different character as it heads back to Crackington Haven along the wildly undulating cliff where millennia of earth processes are exposed.

On a warm summer's day, it's a joy to sit outside The Cabin and gaze up at the cliffs as you cool down with a smoothie or tuck into a cream tea. Should the weather be disagreeable, there's ample seating inside—and hot soup on the menu.

Tea and scones

▶ The Cabin Café at a glance

Open: Daily, 9am-5pm
Food and specialities: Homemade burgers, salad bowls, soups, pasties, sandwiches and paninis. Breakfasts, including full vegetarian option, until 11am. Food is also available to take away.
Beverages: Teas and coffee from local suppliers; soft drinks including smoothies and milk-shakes
Outside: Large outdoor dining area
Dogs: Dogs welcome inside and out

The Walk

1. At the end of the **car park** furthest from the road, join a path heading up to the left. Turn right at the road. After 240 metres, turn right along a track in front of a detached house. Nearing the end of the track, go through a gate on the left to continue on a narrower path along the **woodland edge**. Turn right at the road and, in a few metres, go left to join a trail climbing very steeply through the trees. Turn right along the next road and, after 580 metres, go left at a **crossroads**—signed 'Widemouth Bay'.

2. At the bottom of a short drop, cross the **footbridge** on your left, go through the small gate and bear right for just a few strides. Head up the rough slope to the left and then, back out in the open, ascend the pathless, grass slope ahead (north-north-west). At the top of the first rise, cross the stile between two large gates and walk with the fence on your right. After the next gate, join a rising track and then turn right along a surfaced lane. Turn left at the T-junction.

3. Having walked this road for 420 metres, take the broad track on the right. You've now turned your back on the lovely sea views you've been enjoying from time to time since leaving Crackington Haven, but we'll be seeing more of the ocean later… About 320 metres beyond the

Walk 2 – **The Cabin Café**, Crackington Haven ♦ 15

Carpets of fragrant bluebells edge the clifftop paths

buildings at **Trengayor**, and just before a metal gate across the track, enter the Woodland Trust's glorious **Millook Valley** site via the gate on the left. The path heads downhill, fords a tributary **stream** and continues through **bluebell woods** beside the gently meandering **Millook Water**. Bear right at a fork, quickly crossing a **wooden footbridge**.

4. Turn left after a kissing-gate and pass to the right of a **cottage**. About 70 metres after joining its access lane, you'll reach a fingerpost at a crossing of routes. Take the narrow trail heading across the open ground on your left— signed Millook. Re-entering the **woods**, continue downstream. Cross the next **footbridge**, near another **solitary cottage**, and then continue in roughly the same direction along a broad track.

5. This eventually leads to a quiet road above **Millook Haven**. Turn left. Having walked the asphalt for almost 300 metres, climbing all the while, go through a gap in the hedgerow on the right to head out along the **top of the cliffs**. Looking back along the coast from here, you can see distinctive chevron folding in the rocks once more before you go through a gate and are faced with a choice of routes. The path to the right heads to a **viewpoint** above **Black Rock**, but the main route goes left, dropping into **Crackington Haven**. Turn right at the road and, almost immediately, take the surfaced path on the left to retrace your steps to the car park to complete the walk ♦

Stunted oaks

Forget all those images you have of towering old oak trees; the cliffs at Dizzard are covered in oaks that, because of the battering they receive from Atlantic winds, are unable to grow more than a few metres high. They're an unusual sight. This stunted woodland is also renowned for the many species of lichen that grow on the trees, including several that are unique to Cornwall and Devon.

The light and airy modern tearooms at Boscastle

BOSCASTLE

Boscastle Farm Shop & Café

A magnificent clifftop hike followed by a walk through a beautiful, wooded valley

walk 3

What to expect:
Cliffs; field paths; quiet roads; woodland

Distance/Time: 8.5 kilometres/5½ miles. Allow 2¼-2¾ hours

Start: Cob Web pay-and-display car park in Boscastle (with PC)

Grid ref: SX 100 912

Ordnance Survey Map: Explorer 111, *Bude, Boscastle & Tintagel*

Café: Boscastle Farm Shop and Café, Hillsborough Farm, Boscastle PL35 0HH | 01840 250827 | www.boscastlefarmshop.co.uk

Walk outline: Leaving Boscastle, this walk first heads out on to the cliffs to the north-east of the pretty harbour village. Every twist and turn of the spectacular coast path will have you reaching for your camera and, although you're not on the cliffs for long, these are a few kilometres you'll want to savour. The second half of the walk then heads inland along quiet lanes to join a woodland path through the tranquil Valency Valley.

Extend your time on the cliffs by stopping off at Boscastle Farm Shop and Café. This is a great spot where the home-made quiches, cakes and desserts on display will leave mouths watering. If none of that tempts you, there's lots more besides.

Tempting menu

▶ Boscastle Farm Shop and Café at a glance

Open: Daily, 9am-4pm
Food and specialities: Sandwiches, toasties, burgers, tasty quiches, homity pie and various takes on a ploughman's lunch. Breakfasts, including kippers and vegetarian options, until 11.45am. Much of the meat used is home reared.
Beverages: Teas, coffee and soft drinks from local suppliers; milkshakes and fresh fruit smoothies; wines and Cornish beers and ciders
Outside: Large outdoor dining area
Dogs: Dogs in outdoor area only

The Walk

1. From the **car park** entrance, turn left along the road, soon passing a few **shops and cafés**. Just before the **bridge**, take the lane on the right, following the **River Valency** down towards the **harbour mouth**. *In August 2004, during torrential rain, a flash flood came raging through Boscastle, destroying several buildings and carrying dozens of vehicles out to sea. Helicopters had to be used to rescue about 150 people who were left stranded on top of their homes and cars. Thankfully, no one was seriously hurt.* Just after the **National Trust shop** and the **Museum of Witchcraft and Magic**, take the surfaced lane climbing to the right. Beyond some **cottages**, the way ahead narrows. Having ignored a path dropping down to the harbour, bear right at a fork to begin climbing. Look behind from time to time because this path provides an excellent perspective on Boscastle's unusual curving harbour, safely cradled between two natural headlands.

2. At the **crest of the ridge**, there is a path heading left to the airy **viewpoint** overlooking Penally Point, but our route goes right—through the gate. On reaching some wooden barriers, go through the gate on the right. Walk beside the wall on your left for about

© Crown copyright and/or database right. All rights reserved. Licence number AC0000833184

The River Valency near the sea at Boscastle

30 metres and then bear left through a gap in said wall, quickly followed by a kissing-gate. Follow the line of the wall on the left to pass through another gate that brings you back out on the **exposed cliff** again.

3. Watch for a gap in the wall on your right in a short while. This provides access to a fenced path that leads up to **Boscastle Farm Shop and Café** at **Hillsborough**. Beyond the turning for the farm, descend a long **flight of steps** to cross a **bridge** above the **Pentargon Waterfall**, which is briefly visible on the climb out of this valley. The next part of the walk heads out across beautiful **Beeny Cliff**. *Thomas Hardy, better known as a Dorset-based novelist, once wrote a poem about these cliffs. He met his first wife, Emma, in this area of Cornwall when he was working at nearby St Juliot's Church as a young architect's assistant. He wrote several poems about her, and about this area, after she died in 1912.*

As the path cuts across the cliff, with the ground dropping away steeply to the sea directly below, some walkers may find this section a little unnerving, particularly in windy weather. If that's the case, there is an alternative, higher path. This can be

The sheltered harbour at Boscastle

accessed via a gate in a dip soon after the initial climb from the little valley. (This rejoins the main route near Fire Beacon Point.)

4. The main route climbs to a **bench** overlooking **Fire Beacon Point** and heads east.

5. About 600 metres beyond the bench, you'll reach a kissing-gate at the top of a short, grassy rise. Don't go through it; instead, turn right, walking with the fence on your left. There is a faint trail through the grass. Later enclosed by hedges on either side, the path leads to a road near **North Lodge**. Turn right here.

6. Having dipped and climbed, you'll come out on to the **B3263**. Turn right and then, in just a few metres, go left along a dead-end lane that provides some lovely views of the rolling farmland and its woods. The lane climbs slightly before plummeting, via a series of switchbacks, into the gorgeous valley at **Newmills**.

7. A few metres after passing a driveway for **Elm Cottage** on the left, the way ahead splits. Bear right, along the rough track. Beyond a gate and a cottage, a narrow path continues through the woods. The sound of birdsong and the rush of the water accompany you as the path heads downstream with the **River Valency,** always keeping to the north bank. Dense oak woods cover the valley slopes, while, in spring, the woodland floor is bedecked with bluebells and wild garlic. In summer, a variety of butterfly species, including the rare pearl-bordered fritillary, flit among the wildflowers in the meadows bordering the river. After about 1.6 kilometres, on nearing **Boscastle**, the path splits. Bear right here, soon re-entering the car park where the walk started to complete the walk. ♦

Witchcraft

Boscastle has been home to a museum dedicated to witchcraft and folk magic since 1960. Formerly located on the Isle of Man, it was originally run by a folk magician called Cecil Williamson. Today, it houses one of the largest collections of its type in Europe and has exhibits devoted to witch trials, alchemy and Freemasonry, including a chalice owned by the controversial early 20th-century occultist Aleister Crowley.

24 ♦ TOP 10 WALKS **NORTH CORNWALL: TEA SHOP WALKS**

Charlie's cafe and deli, in the centre of Tintagel

TINTAGEL

walk 4

Charlie's

Step back in time to wander through a landscape where history and legend collide

What to expect:
Clifftop path; valley trails, including boardwalk; road without footway; fields

Distance/Time: 10 kilometres/6½ miles. Allow 3¼ - 3¾ hours

Start: King Arthur's Arms Inn, Tintagel

Grid ref: SX 056 885

Ordnance Survey Map: Explorer 111, *Bude, Boscastle & Tintagel*

Café: Charlie's, Fore Street, Tintagel PL34 0DA | 01840 779500
www.charlies.cafe

Walk outline: It's hard to single out one highlight on this walk—there are so many. The spectacularly located, clifftop ruins of Tintagel Castle are passed close to the start of the walk, but even after this the coastal scenery remains breathtaking. We head inland through a steep-sided ravine in the National Trust's Rocky Valley. And that's not all… Beyond this, the route heads to St Nectan's Glen for a stroll through peaceful woodland.

Charlie's is located in a 14th-century cottage in the heart of Tintagel. Part-café, part-deli, this award-winning business offers cosy indoor areas as well as a large courtyard where customers can tuck into food that is largely sourced locally. Seasonal menus.

Cornish ale

▶ Charlie's at a glance

Open: 10am-5pm (4pm in winter), closed Sun
Food and specialities: Sandwiches on homemade sourdough baked daily, salads, waffles and hot dishes such as soups and lentil dhal; Cornish cream teas served with tea, coffee or, for a special occasion, Prosecco
Beverages: An emphasis on local suppliers, including Tintagel bottled beers, Cornish gins and various soft drinks
Outside: Large courtyard
Dogs: Outside only and on short leads

The Walk

1. With your back to the **King Arthur's Arms**, turn right along the road and then left down **Vicarage Hill**. As the lane later climbs, it bends right. Cross a stile beside a large gate to the left here. Follow the track swinging right – up to another gate and stile. Beyond this, walk with the hedgerow on your left for about 60 metres and then follow the faint trail across the middle of the field to a stile. An enclosed path then leads on to a rough track which, in turn, leads to a surfaced lane. Turn sharp right.

© Crown copyright and/or database right. All rights reserved. Licence number AC0000833184

2. After about 225 metres on the asphalt, turn left along a lane with a **National Trust 'Glebe Cliff' sign** and a **YHA arrow** at the start of it. At a fork, bear right. This rough track soon swings right and then joins the route of the coast path. As the wide path then heads up towards the **church**, keep left along a narrower trail. Bear left at the next path junction. The impressive **footbridge** ahead links the mainland and **The Island**, on which **Tintagel Castle**'s ruins stand. Just beyond the **ticket office**, turn left, descending steps.

3. Reaching a lane, turn left to pass a **café** and **shop**. Cross the **stream** to climb back on to the cliffs. After a **small**

Tintagel Castle is connected to the mainland via a new 'sky' bridge

bridge, bear right at a fork in the path. At the next **waymarker post**, continue straight across —on the trail nearest the cliff edge.

4. As you pass through a wall, entering National Trust land at **Willapark**, turn right. An undulating section begins soon—typical of the coast path in this part of Cornwall. Descend a **flight of steps** and cross a **footbridge** just above the small cove at **Bossiney Haven**. When the tide retreats, a sandy beach is revealed. A path heads inland in a short while, but continue on the cliffs for now.

5. A few metres after a **bench**, the path drops into **Rocky Valley**. Here, a crystal-clear stream tumbles down through a narrow, steep-sided ravine. The path forks just before a **bridge**. Bear right here to continue upstream through this idyllic valley. Cross to the east bank at the next bridge—near the picturesque ruins of **Trewethet Mill**. *There's some Bronze Age rock art on the rocks in an alcove to the left just after the mill.* The path crosses back at Trevillett Mill. Ascend the holiday cottages' access lane and turn left along the **B3263**. Being careful on the bends, walk the road for about 600 metres.

Boardwalk through St Nectan's Glen

6. Opposite the bus shelter in **Trethevey**, turn right along a rough track signed to "St Nectan's Waterfall". Drawing level with **St Piran's Well**, keep left along the signposted byway, climbing steadily. (Ignore the lane on the right to 'St Nectan's Glen'.) At the top of the rise, follow the track round to the right.

7. When you reach the **Tree of Life Café**, drop right. In a few more strides, near the **St Nectan's Glen ticket office,** go sharp right to keep to the public right of way descending through **dense woodland**. Having crossed **two bridges** in the valley bottom, you'll reach a path junction at a third bridge. Cross this and walk uphill through the trees towards **Halgrabon**. Emerging from the woods, head up to the bungalow on the left and continue beside its fence.

8. Cross the stile and turn left along the road. You'll see one footpath to the right in 90 metres. Ignore this, but then cross the stile on the right 30 metres later. Walk towards the buildings on the far side of the field. Cross two stiles in quick succession and follow the gravel driveway to the road. Turn right.

9. After 130 metres on the asphalt, turn left to reach a gate set back from the road. Cross the stile next to this and head west-north-west across the field. Once over the stile, go through the small gate ahead and walk west. In the next field, swing slightly right of your previous line to reach the road via a stile. Turn left to walk back into Tintagel. There's pavement most of the way and you'll find **Charlie's** on the right soon after the mini roundabout. ♦

King Arthur at Tintagel

The site of Tintagel Castle was a stronghold for local rulers from the middle of the fifth century onwards, and played a role in trade with the Mediterranean. In the 12th century, Geoffrey of Monmouth named it as the birthplace of King Arthur and it was this that led Richard, Earl of Cornwall to build his castle here a century later. The site remains closely linked with Arthurian legend today.

Woods Café has a substantial outdoor seating area

CARDINHAM WOODS

walk 5

Woods Café

A ramble through dense woodland and a visit to a historic church

What to expect: *Good forest paths; roads; fields*

Distance/Time: 10 kilometres/6 miles. Allow 3 - 3½ hours

Start: Forestry England's Cardinham Woods pay-and-display car park (with PC)

Grid ref: SX 099 667

Ordnance Survey Map: Explorer 109, *Bodmin Moor*

Café: Woods Café, Cardinham Woods, Bodmin PL30 4AL | 01208 78111 | www.woodscafe.co.uk

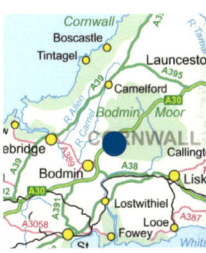

Walk outline: Forestry England's Cardinham Woods is set in rolling Cornish countryside a few kilometres east of Bodmin. These sprawling woods, consisting of both broadleaf and conifer species, hug the banks of a steep-sided valley through which Cardinham Water and its tributaries flow. This walk explores the woodland, particularly beautiful in spring and autumn, and then heads out to the village of Cardinham, home to a church with ancient stone crosses in its grounds.

Find a table in the shade of the trees and tuck into delicious home-made food from the family-run Woods Café. Cakes and scones are baked daily and, wherever possible, local ingredients are used. There's also some seating inside this cosy woodland cottage.

Sunny courtyard

▶ Woods Café at a glance

Open: Daily, 10.30am-4pm
Food and specialities: Soup, doorstop sandwiches, warm ciabattas and simple, hearty specials, seasonal salads; healthy kids' lunch box includes sandwiches, fruit and carrot sticks
Beverages: Locally roasted coffee, teas, hot chocolates; soft fruit drinks
Outside: Large outdoor dining area
Dogs: Dogs welcome

Sunlight illuminates one of the broad forest paths

The Walk

1. From the **car park**, cross the **pedestrian bridge** into the **Woods Café** area. Bear left and then go right at a junction, keeping right when paths go off in various directions. This broad track quickly passes directly above the café. The first 1.3 kilometres is fairly level as the route heads up the valley through **mixed woodland**. Staying on the west bank of **Cardinham Water** for now, ignore the first bridge across it.

2. As the route then splits, bear right to cross a second bridge, known as **Ladyvale Bridge**, and immediately turn left. The route now begins a steady ascent through **Deviock Wood**, later swinging right to continue up beside a little **stream**. Turn right at the next path junction. Keep straight on along a grassier route, ignoring a mountain bike trail followed quickly by a walkers' trail on the right.

3. Leave Forestry England land at a stile. The trail continues through woodland *that's awash with wildflowers in spring and summer before donning its autumn glory later in the year.* Leaving the trees, swing up to the right, through long grass, passing less than 10 metres to the left of a power pole. After a wooden farm gate, turn left. This concrete track leads to a quiet road, where you turn right.

4. After 1 kilometre, the road drops sharply to cross a **stream**. On the other side, climb the stile in the trees on the right. Head straight up the field, aiming just to the right of the group of buildings in the top part of the **village of Cardinham**. Go through the gate and join a lane that takes you out past the **church** to the road. *The church is well worth a visit, home to several interesting internal features and two ancient crosses*. Turn right along the road.

5. When the road bends right (after about 400 metres), go through the gate on the left. Maintain a straight line through the grounds of this house, passing along the gravel **driveway**, through a gap in the bamboo and then down a rough, stony path to a gate. Once through this, the **old bridleway** heads down through sparse woodland. Cross a **bridge** and then head uphill beside the field boundary on the left. Pass through a couple more gates and to the right of a rundown **old farm building**. Cross potentially muddy ground to join a rough track that leads to a lane. Turn right here.

© Crown copyright and/or database right. All rights reserved. Licence number AC0000833184

Bluebell woods near Cardinham

6. Go through the gate on the left immediately after the cottage. The enclosed path leads to a gate, beyond which you enter a field. Follow the line of the fence on your left uphill. Contrary to what the right of way appears to do on the map, the gate providing access to the road is a few metres in from the field corner. Turn right along the road.

7. Take the next turning on the right and then cross diagonally right to join a rough track. (Be careful because there are two tracks heading in roughly the same direction here. You should take the more northerly of the two; not the signposted bridleway.) When the track splits at a pair of gates, choose the right-hand option to re-enter **Cardinham Woods**.

8. Bear left at a clear fork and you'll soon see the remains of the **Wheal Glynn mine** on the right, its **chimney** eerily swamped by ivy, blending in with the tall trees surrounding it.

Wheal Glynn is one of the many mines that sprung up locally during the Crimean War when it became difficult to import certain metals. Known as 'bubble mines' many, like this one, lasted only a few years and closed after making huge losses. Lead, iron, copper and silver were mined here. Before long the path swings right to come back down the western side of this little ravine.

Another route joins from the left and Wheal Glynn reappears on your right.

9. In the valley bottom, keep straight ahead as you join a broad track coming in from the right. Just after passing **Range Cottage**, bear right along a broad path running parallel with the road. This leads back into the **car park** via the **rangers' hut**, **public toilets** and **dog wash area** to complete the walk. ♦

Ancient crosses

The grounds of St Meubred's Church, Cardinham, contains two crosses. The wheel-headed cross outside the porch dates from the ninth century and features ornate Norse-style carving. Older still is the monument at the churchyard's south-east entrance. Topped by a medieval cross, the stone shaft dates from the late sixth or early seventh century. Bearing a Latin inscription that translates as 'Rancorus son of Mesgus', it is thought to be a gravestone

Home-made cakes are a speciality at Cherry Trees

PADSTOW

Cherry Trees

After a stroll along the Camel Trail, explore the pretty countryside on either side of a little creek

walk 6

What to expect: *Cycle path; meadows; potentially muddy marshland; woods; town*

Distance/Time: 9 kilometres/5½ miles. Allow 2¼-2¾ hours

Start: Old Custom House Hotel, Padstow harbour

Grid ref: SW 919 753

Ordnance Survey Map: Explorer 106, *Newquay & Padstow*

Café: Cherry Trees, West Quay, Padstow PL28 8AQ | 01841 532 934
www.cherry-trees-christmas.myshopify.com

Walk outline: It's hard to believe it when you set off from busy Padstow, but this is one of the quietest walks in this book. You probably won't believe it when you're on the Camel Trail either, popular with cyclists and walkers alike, but then you reach Little Petherick Creek… We go up one side of this tranquil side valley and down the other, walking on the marshland beside the creek, through fields and in and out of serene woodland.

Whoever said 'good things come in small packages' must've had the friendly Cherry Trees in mind. This tiny coffee house serves up excellent brunches, lunches and homemade cakes from compact, but buzzing premises overlooking Padstow's sparkling harbour.

Superb coffee

▶ Cherry Trees at a glance

Open: Daily, 9am-5pm
Food and specialities: Assorted brunches, pancakes, burritos, Buddha bowls, sandwiches, toasties and, of course, a variety of pasties. Kids' lunch bags. All food also available to take away
Beverages: Locally roasted coffee, teas, milk-shakes and assorted fruit juices
Outside: None
Dogs: No dogs inside, please

The Walk

1. With your back to the **Old Custom House Hotel**, turn right along the road. Pass one **car park**. Walk between **bollards** on the left and keep to the right of the building housing **Rick Stein's Cookery School**. Head to the far end of this **larger car park**, walking to the right of the big blue **boatyard building** to join the **Camel Trail**, a multi-use path that follows the disused railway. As you later cross the old **railway bridge** over **Little Petherick Creek**, *watch for oystercatchers, curlews and egrets where this tidal tributary enters the River Camel.*

2. On the **east bank**, take the rough track climbing right. When this becomes a surfaced lane, cross the stile on the right. Walking south-west across the field, look to the right for good views back over the bridge you just crossed and down the River Camel. After a step stile, continue in the same direction. Go through a kissing-gate and cross the track diagonally left to climb a stile. Descend the field and, after a **footbridge**, drop on to the potentially muddy ground beside the **tidal creek**. This can be slippery when wet.

Walk 6 – **Cherry Trees**, Padstow ♦ 39

Looking down Little Petherick Creek towards the River Camel

3. In just a few metres, head up the lane on the left. After 80m on the asphalt, go sharp right through a large gate. Take just a few strides along the **driveway** and then climb the **steps** and stile on the left. In the meadow, bear right, following the hedgerow on your right. Cross a stile into a second meadow and continue with the hedgerow. Another stile leads to an enclosed section of path which emerges on a lane at the edge of the **creek** at the secluded hamlet of **Sea Mills.** Turn left. *There used to be a tidal lagoon here. This captured the water from a rising tide and used it to power a gristmill.*

4. On drawing level with **Mill Cottage**, take the path signposted to the right. This first heads west along the edge of the marshy ground and then swings south. Having walked south for about 550m, the path leaves the increasingly muddy ground and takes a higher route heading in exactly the same direction. (There is an old fingerpost indicating where the path heads up.) Continue through the trees at first. After two step stiles in quick succession, walk along the bottom edge of two meadows. Beyond a **bridge** and a gate, bear right to walk along the field edge and then cross yet another

Padstow harbour and waterfront

step stile on the far side. Walk across this marshy ground, cross a **footbridge** and bear right. Follow the wastewater treatment works' track to the **A389**.

5. Turn right at the road in **Little Petherick** and then take the lane on the right immediately after crossing the creek. You're now following the **Saints' Way**, waymarked back to Padstow. Beyond **Quay House**, when the lane heads uphill, take the path to the left of the white building. This climbs through **bluebell woods**, taking a higher line than the route on the **creek's east bank**. Leaving the woods, keep straight ahead with the hedgerow. Follow it to the left and then, drawing level with a gate, turn right. Heading downhill, fork left on open ground. Go through a gate, cross **two bridges** across marshy ground and go through another gate to climb again. *You're soon looking down on the creek from the edge of fields that, in early spring, are full of cultivated daffodils.* After three stiles, turn left and descend to cross a **footbridge** over another arm of the creek.

6. Climb the other side and, as you emerge into the open, walk straight across the field (north-east). Go left at a **water trough**, walking with a fence on your right. Negotiate a gate and stile on your right and then turn left to descend towards Padstow. After a gate, follow the track downhill.

7. Turn right at a surfaced lane. Go straight over a road junction—along **Dennis Road**. Turn left at a T-junction and immediately right. Just after **St Petroc's Bistro** (on the left), take the narrow lane on the right. This drops to the **harbour**. Turn right to return to the start point, or, to visit **Cherry Trees** beside the harbour, go left. ♦

Saints' Way
The Saints' Way is a 44-kilometre long-distance path that goes coast to coast across Cornwall—from Padstow in the north to Fowey in the south. It traces the route early Christian pilgrims might have taken on their way from Wales and Ireland to important religious sites in continental Europe. Together with the St Michael's Way, it forms part of the 201-kilometre Cornish Celtic Way from St Germans to St Michael's Mount.

The barbecue terrace overlooks Trevone beach

TREVONE

Trevone Beach Stores & Café

A hike to a windswept headland followed by a stroll beside the estuary into Padstow

walk 7

What to expect:
Clifftop path; fields; lanes; town paths

Distance/Time: 12.5 kilometres/8 miles. Allow 3¼ - 3¾ hours

Start: Pay-and-display car park at Trevone Bay (with PC)

Grid ref: SW 891 759

Ordnance Survey Map: Explorer 106, *Newquay & Padstow*

Café: Trevone Beach Stores and Café, Trevone Beach Complex, near Padstow PL28 8QY. Tel: 01841 520275 trevonebaybeach@gmail.com

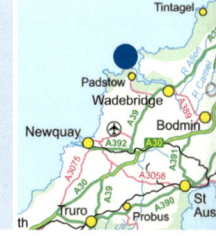

Walk outline: Low cliffs gradually give way to more rugged scenery as this route heads north from Trevone on to the headland guarding the western entrance to the mouth of the River Camel. Rounding Stepper Point, views of the Atlantic Ocean are replaced by beaches, dunes and woods fringing the estuary. The route then calls in at Padstow before cutting across the neck of the peninsula to return to Trevone.

Sit on the terrace, sipping a cool beer and gaze out beyond the palm tree to the golden sands in the bay. A Caribbean island perhaps? Or the beach café at Trevone on the Cornish coast? Time your visit carefully and enjoy a pizza from the wood-fired oven.

Cosy café

▶ Trevone Beach Stores & Café at a glance

Open: Daily, 8.30am-9pm (summer); 9-4pm (winter)
Food and specialities: Breakfasts, including baps and full vegetarian option, until 11.30am; simple lunches and a range of tasty pizzas cooked in a wood-fired oven. Smaller children's sizes also available
Beverages: Teas, coffees and soft drinks; licensed bar serves beers, wines and spirits
Outside: Large outdoor dining area, some tables under cover
Dogs: Well-behaved dogs welcome

The Walk

1. Standing in the pay-and-display **car park** with the **café** on your right, drop on to the lane below and turn left. Passing around the back of the **beach**, keep left and walk behind the **Lifeguards hut**. As the lane then bends right, climb the steps on the left to set out along the **coast path**.

An RSPB sign indicates this area is managed as a sanctuary for ground-nesting birds such as skylarks and corn buntings, so walkers should keep to the close-cropped grass along the top of the low cliffs. Watch too for wheatears in summer as well as seabirds, such as fulmars and kittiwakes, nesting on the cliffs.

The **Round Hole** is soon passed, *a 25 metre-deep, almost perfectly circular collapsed sea cave. Unfenced and with steep sides, it has been the scene of several accidents over the years.* Keep to the seaward side of some walls in a short while. As you stride out over the grassy cliff tops, *the scenery becomes increasingly rugged with tiny, rocky coves biting into the coastline and stacks standing just offshore.*

2. Two streams are crossed near **Middle Merope Island**. After the second of these, head straight up the steep slope ahead to regain the **clifftop path**

© Crown copyright and/or database right. All rights reserved. Licence number AC0000833184

A gull's-eye view of the Daymark on Stepper Point

heading roughly north. The prominent **Daymark tower** that crowns the headland soon appears, drawing walkers on.

3. After a fairly long level stretch, pass above **Butter Hole**, *the sand on the beach below the colour of… well… butter.* The coast path then swings north-east, above the blowhole known as **Pepper Hole** before it makes its way up to the **Daymark**. *Built in the 1830s, this served as a navigational aid to sailors entering the Camel estuary during daylight hours.*

4. Don't cross the wall immediately behind the tower; instead, continue over the tiny lip of rock directly ahead and walk downhill. A **waymarker post** at the bottom of the drop then indicates when you should swing right to cross the wall. The route passes below the **Lookout Station** at **Stepper Point** and then swings south. *You're now looking straight up the broad mouth of the River Camel. There are substantial sandy beaches in the river mouth, as well as some small areas of dunes and patches of woodland.*

5. Join a surfaced path at **Hawker's Cove** and then follow a lane away from the buildings for about 100 metres. When it then bends right, take the path on the

The broad sandy beach at Hawker's Cove, on the Camel Estuary

left. On nearing a small **creek** at **Harbour Cove**, keep to the clearest path. This then bends left at a **waymarker post** to reach a crossing of routes. Go straight over and cross the **bridge**. Climb the steps and turn left after the gate, walking along a field edge. The path then swings left, over a short section of **boardwalk**. Turn right at the T-junction and, in about 40m, take the trail on the left. As you draw level with a concrete building at **St George's Cove**, ignore the trail to the left and then bear right at a clear fork.

6. Beyond the **war memorial** and **benches**, fork left to descend towards Padstow. The path drops on to the **North Quay**, a busy spot on warm summer days. Bear right beside the **ice-cream parlour** and follow this narrow lane round to a road. Turn right.

7. At the top of the rise, take the road climbing right (**Cross Street**). Turn right again at a T-junction, with the **Dower House** on your left. About 500m after passing **Prideaux Place** on the edge of Padstow, turn left over a stile—signed Crugmeer. The trail heads half-right (north-west) across this field and six more, crossing several stiles and one farm track along the way.

8. Turn left along a lane at **Crugmeer**, go right at the road and, almost immediately, take the lane on the left. As you pass the site of the former **Padstow Airfield**, used in World War One, the beach at Harlyn Bay can be seen across the water. Beyond the farm buildings at **Porthmissen**, the lane descends steeply to **Trevone**. Pass around the back of the **Lifeguards hut** and then retrace your steps to the **car park** where the walk started. ♦

Foodie heaven

Wandering around Padstow, you can't help but notice there are a lot of places to eat. The celebrity chef Rick Stein opened his first restaurant here in 1975, specialising in seafood, and now runs several businesses in and around the harbour, including a cookery school. His links with the town have led to it being nicknamed Padstein. The Michelin-starred chef Paul Ainsworth also has restaurants here.

The Walk

1. From the **car park**, go right along the road and right again at the T-junction. Opposite the **Spar shop**, turn right along Polbreen Lane. Go straight across at a road, along **Whitworth Close**. Emerging on the next road, keep straight ahead for a few strides and then take the path behind the bench to the right – signed to 'St Agnes Beacon'. Quickly go left at the wall corner. Turn right when you reach a track.

2. Go straight across a surfaced lane. Out on the open hillside, walk beside the fence on the right. Soon after a stile, take the path on the right and follow it up, past a bench, to the **toposcope** on **St Agnes Beacon** (630ft/192m).

As well as enjoying superb views out along the north Cornish coast, this viewpoint provides a sense of just how important the tin mining industry was to this area, with the remains of the industry dotted throughout the countryside.

3. Descending the other side of the beacon, ignore a trail to the right and then, with the coast beckoning, fork left. At a road, head diagonally left, still aiming for the sea. Immediately after a small **breezeblock building** (*a sentry box used in World War Two*), head around

© Crown copyright and/or database right. All rights reserved. Licence number AC0000833184

On the coast path between Portreath and Godrevy

the side of the gate over to the left. Cross the **steps** at the end of the track and continue on an obvious path. At a crossing of routes, keep straight on.

4. Reaching the road-end **car park**, head left along the clear path and quickly take the path on the right, swinging round on to the exposed **clifftop**. So begins another magnificent section of the **South West Coast Path**. Keep left at an early fork to remain on the cliff edge. Some people might find this path a little vertiginous, especially on windy days.

There are trails heading back inland at various points should you feel it's too much; otherwise keep left. The path soon eases its way around the tip of **St Agnes Head**. As you later round **Newdowns Head**, *another spectacular scene opens out ahead, including part of Trevaunance Cove. Dozens of caves bite into the rugged cliffs north-east of Trevellas Porth while, offshore, seabirds are drawn to the numerous stacks and tiny, jagged islands.*

5. Eventually, having descended some steps, you'll drop to broad, stony path

The 'Cornwall and West Devon Mining Landscape' is a World Heritage site

just above **Trevaunance Cove**. Turn right and walk around the side of a metal gate to join a surfaced lane. After about 160 metres, go through a **gap in the wall** on the left and descend the steps. A path brings you out on to the lane leading down into the cove. Turn right along this and then take the **coast path** signposted on the left just before **The Driftwood Spars** pub. (Alternatively, to visit Café Q, continue up the road for a further 250 metres.) The coast path climbs back on to the cliffs. Soon after passing some spoil heaps, fork right, keeping away from the unfenced cliff edge. Go left at a second fork and then straight over a crossing of routes to begin a steep descent.

6. Turn left along a lane for 65 metres and then take the track through the large gate on the right. The route quickly passes an **old engine house**. Pass to the right of a set of blue gates to follow a narrow trail beside a fence. This heads gently uphill through the steep-sided **Trevellas Coombe**. You might find yourself sharing the path with the stream after heavy rain, but only for a few metres; generally, the pleasant stream keeps within its channel as it makes its way to the sea. At a junction, turn right to cross the **footbridge** and go left along the lane.

7. Go right at the road and take the next

turning on the left – signed 'Portreath and Porthtowan'. Almost immediately, turn right. About 150 metres after a sharp right bend, take the narrow lane rising left. Turn right at the road and then take the next turning on the left, with the **Rosemundy House Hotel** on the corner. Go right at the main road and then left along **Trelawny Road** to return to the **car park** to complete the walk. ♦

World Heritage site

The St Agnes area forms part of the World Heritage site known as the Cornwall and West Devon Mining Landscape. Copper and tin were mined here in the 18th and 19th centuries, with more than 30,000 people employed in Cornwall alone when the industry was at its peak. It was recognised by Unesco in 2006 in recognition of the substantial remains that are dotted about the region, including the much-photographed engine houses.

The Hub enjoys two outside seating areas

PORTREATH

The Hub

A varied ramble taking in a wooded valley, a country park and magnificent cliffs

walk 9

What to expect:
Roads; clear paths; country park; cliffs

Distance/Time: 8.5 kilometres/5 miles. Allow 2½-3 hours

Start: Seafront pay-and-display car park in Portreath, opposite The Hub

Grid ref: SW 654 453

Ordnance Survey Map: Explorer 104 *Redruth & St Agnes*

Café: The Hub, The Sea Front, Portreath, TR16 4NN Tel: 01209 844666 www.thehubportreath.com

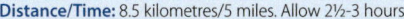

Walk outline: This walk starts off with a gentle ramble up a tree-lined valley that is pure joy in spring when wildflowers cover the woodland floor. This is followed by a long section through a popular country park, the largest area of woodland in west Cornwall. Heading out to Basset's Cove, the outing culminates in a short, but very sweet section of the South West Coast Path over the top of high cliffs where walkers are able to look down on wave-battered stacks and islands.

Whether you sit indoors or out, there's a laid-back feel to The Hub. The coffee's good, the fresh Cornish crab sandwiches are great and, all the while, you can hear the sea washing up against the beach on the other side of the road. If the sun's shining, it's perfect!

Home-made pastries

▶ The Hub at a glance

Open: Daily, 9am-4pm
Food and specialities: All-day breakfasts, including vegan options; paninis, salads, jacket potatoes and pizzas. Children's menu. For the sweet-toothed, there are waffles, cakes, pastries and ice-cream.
Beverages: Hot drinks, smoothies, milkshakes, freakshakes, beer, wine and spirits
Outside: Two outdoor seating areas
Dogs: Well-behaved dogs welcome

The Walk

1. Leave the **car park** and walk east along the road ahead—with **The Hub** on the right. When the road bends left, cross the bridge on the right and then veer left under the **old bridge**. Keep right at a fork and, when the lane ends, join the surfaced path on the right.

2. After a **bridge**, the path makes its way steadily uphill through a pleasant, **wooded valley**. Soon after crossing to the western side of the **stream**, fork right. Emerging from the trees, keep right and then bear right along a stony track. Join a surfaced lane and then follow a path round to the left to join a concrete track.

3. Reaching a road, look to your right and you'll see a gate to a property called **Ravenshaw**. Take the path to left of this. At the next junction, turn right and then follow the path left. This crosses two tracks and ends at a surfaced lane where you turn left. Go left again at the road and, in just 30m, take the track between the **stone gateposts** on the right. (The thatched **East Lodge** is on the right here.)

4. Soon after a path joins from the right, you find yourself walking under a canopy provided by a narrow **band of tall pines**. Entering thicker woodland again, keep straight ahead, initially following signs for Coombe. As the path swings left, turn right—signed 'North Cliffs car park'. Keep to the clearest path, soon swinging left. Go right at a waymarked T-junction. Ignoring a path to the left early on, keep straight ahead, following **green and pink**

© Crown copyright and/or database right. All rights reserved. Licence number AC0000833184

The old lighthouse at Portreath, known as the Pepperpot

waymarkers until they indicate a left turn at a crossing of routes. Keep straight on here, soon leaving the trees.

5. Turn left at the road and then take the broad track on the right. This ends at the **Basset's Cove car park**. Head right to join the **coast path** along the cliff-top. The path dips and climbs twice. On the way out of the second dip, look back to see the stream become a **waterfall** as it plummets into the cove below. Soon after **Portreath** appears, you'll see a path to the right. Ignore this. Keep straight on for now and then swing right to descend steeply. Beyond a kissing-gate, continue downhill and then veer right—up a narrow lane. Turn left at the main road. The **car park** where the walk started is on the left. ♦

Daffodil cultivation

Parts of West Cornwall are awash with daffodils early in the year—not the free-range variety, but cultivated flowers. The county is one of the world's leading suppliers and is estimated to harvest about 900 million stems annually, with the main export markets being Europe and the US. The annual flower crop is estimated to be worth more than £100 million, with bulb sales bringing in a further £10 million per year.

The Dog and Rabbit serves locally roasted coffee

CAPE CORNWALL AND ST JUST

walk 10

Dog and Rabbit Café

A dramatic cliff-top hike with a visit to a quiet Cornish village

What to expect:
Coast path; farmland; good tracks; village

Distance/Time: 9 kilometres/ 5½miles. Allow 2¼ – 2¾ hours

Start: National Trust's Cape Cornwall car park (with PC), TR19 7NN

Grid ref: SW 353 317

Ordnance Survey Map: Explorer 102, *Land's End*

Café: Dog and Rabbit Café, North Row, Saint Just TR19 7LB | 01736 449811

Walk outline: The highlight of this walk is definitely the coastal section, taking in Cape Cornwall and an exciting trail that cuts across the cliff-face, past old mine workings slicing deep into the rock, and with views down to iconic Land's End. It's more than just a coastal ramble though; it also heads inland, across the fields and along delightful lanes, to call in at St Just, a village that provides a taste of what ordinary life is like at this remote, windswept tip of the county.

The Dog and Rabbit is typical of this friendly little village just beyond the tourist honeypots—warm and welcoming. You're guaranteed to find something unusual on the menu, such as jackfruit, and the coffee is always excellent.

Tempting menus

▶ The Dog and Rabbit Café at a glance

Open: Mon-Sat, 9am-4pm
Food and specialities: Soups, sandwiches, exciting salads packed with local organic veg, tasty brunches including traditional English breakfasts and, of course, cakes galore!
Beverages: Assorted teas; single-origin coffee roasted in Cornwall; soft drinks including milkshakes; beers, wines and spirits
Outside: There are a few tables in front of the café
Dogs: Pooches are greeted with a tasty treat

The Walk

1. Walk to the end of the **toilet block** and, leaving the **car park**, go through the gate diagonally opposite. Head half-left, later passing to the right of **St Helen's Oratory**. Climb the **steps** at the wall corner and turn left. Take the next path on the right and follow it up to the **mine chimney** on the **headland**.

2. From the chimney, return to the path junction beside the wall and turn right. Bear left along the track and then, immediately after the gate across it, descend between walls on the right. Go left along an asphalt track and then sharp right, at the next junction. This emerges on a surfaced lane. Follow this until you see a **trig pillar** to the left.

3. Turn right here, soon passing **Ballowall Barrow**. After passing some walled **mine shafts**, the path drops into a tiny, steep-sided valley. Drawing level with a **National Trust sign** on the left, turn sharp right.

4. Go right again at the road and then descend **steps** on the left. After a **footbridge**, the trail heads downstream before

Working boats at Cape Cornwall

joining a wider path from the left. Your coastal journey soon recommences on a wonderful path cutting across the cliff-face, passing several **mine shafts**. At the top of the next little climb, ignore a trail up to the left; continue on the signed coast path. Switch back left, go right at the next junction and then join a **clifftop path** from the left. Soon after a gate in a fence, climb some steps and veer left, away from the coast path, towards a wall. Walk with this on your left. At a trough at the wall corner, continue in the same direction for 80 metres and then watch for unevenly spaced **stepping stones** heading north-east.

5. These lead across wet ground to a kissing-gate. A drier path now heads to the right of the house at **Boscregan**. Join a track heading uphill, passing houses at **Hendra** and **Little Hendra**. About 160 metres beyond the latter, as the track bends right, take the path signposted left—along the field edge. At a kink in the field boundary, keep straight ahead (north-north-east) to pass through a gap (with a **stone gate post** on the left). Maintain your line, crossing one narrow

Sunset over Cape Cornwall near Land's End

field and then, in the next field, keep close to the hedgerow on the left to drop to a power pole. An overgrown trail passes to the right of this and descends.

6. At the bottom of some **steps**, go diagonally left to locate a descending path. (To the left of the gate into **Lower Cot Mill**.) After the next gate, turn right along a **grassy trod**. This crosses a wall and continues between fences. At the top, bear left along a **walled track**. Go straight over at a junction, pass through a wall gap and turn left. This walled path leads on to a lane on the edge of St Just. Go straight over at the next junction— through a gap in the wall. Reaching a road, continue in the same direction, along an alley. Turn left at the **main road**.

7. After passing through the **village centre**, you'll see a **war memorial** on the left. The **Dog and Rabbit Café** is about 70 metres down a side lane on the opposite side of the main road. To continue on the route though, take the road on the left and immediately go right along a narrow lane. Go straight over a crossroads. When the lane swings right, maintain your line by taking the rough track off this bend. At the far end, keep straight ahead, aiming for a metal gate on the far side of the field. Beyond this, walk with the hedgerow on your left across two fields. On the far side of the

Useful Information

Visit North Cornwall
The official tourism website for Cornwall covers everything from accommodation and where to eat to ideas for days out – **www.visitcornwall.com/places/north-cornwall**

Cornwall Area of Outstanding Natural Beauty
The Cornwall AONB covers several stretches of the North Cornwall coast and Bodmin Moor –**www.cornwall-aonb.gov.uk**

Selected Tourist Information Centres

Bodmin Information Centre: Shire Hall, Mount Folly, PL31 2D	01208 76616
Boscastle Visitor Centre (National Trust), The Harbour, PL35 0HD	01840 250010
Bude TIC and Canal Visitor Centre, The Crescent Car Park, EX23 8LE	01288 354240
Padstow TIC, The Mariner's Clock Building, South Quay, PL28 8BL	01841 533449

St Agnes – year-round visitor advice and assistance in 10 businesses across the parish; see **www.visitstagnes.com** for locations

St Just TIC, Market Street, TR19 7HX	01736 788165
Tintagel Visitor Centre, Bossiney Road, PL34 0AJ	01840 779084

Rail Travel
Cornwall's mainline stations include Liskeard, Bodmin Parkway, Lostwithiel, St Austell, Redruth, Truro and Penzance. There are also branch lines that serve the North Cornwall coast, terminating at St Ives and Newquay.
National Rail Enquiries – **www.nationalrail.co.uk** | 03457 484950

Bus Travel
For details of buses serving North Cornwall and to plan journeys, visit **www.travelinesw.com** or phone 0871 200 22 33 (telephone lines are staffed daily, 7am-8pm)

Camping
Cornwall is a popular area for camping, with many sites owned by or affiliated to the Camping and Caravanning Club: 024 7647 5426 | **www.campingandcaravanningclub.co.uk**

econd one, join a track and then turn
eft, passing between the buildings.
• Go right at the road and right along
 track just before the next building.
eep straight on when the vehicle track
bends left. Bear left along the **coast path**, passing above a **cliff-top cottage** and you'll see Cape Cornwall ahead. Turn right at the road and re-enter the **car park** on the left. ♦

Ballowall Barrow

One of many such funerary monuments in this part of Cornwall, Ballowall Barrow dates largely from the Bronze Age although it also contains evidence of late Neolithic burials. When it was discovered under debris from nearby tin mines in the 1870s, archaeologists unearthed several stone-lined chambers, or cists, with pottery and burnt bone in them. Unfortunately, Victorian modifications to the site mean that what visitors see today isn't all prehistoric.